Office Management

A Productivity and Effectiveness Guide

Revised Edition

**Marilyn Manning, Ph.D.
Patricia Haddock**

A Crisp Fifty-Minute™ Series Book

This Fifty-Minute™ book is designed to be "read with a pencil." It is an excellent workbook for self-study as well as classroom learning. All material is copyright-protected and cannot be duplicated without permission from the publisher. *Therefore, be sure to order a copy for every training participant through our Web site, www.courseilt.com.*

Office Management

A Productivity and Effectiveness Guide

Revised Edition

Marilyn Manning, Ph.D.
Patricia Haddock

CREDITS:
Product Manager: **Debbie Woodbury**
Editor: **Charlotte Bosarge**
Production Editor: **Jill Zayszly**
Production Artists: **Nicole Phillips, Rich Lehl, and Betty Hopkins**
Cartoonist: **Ralph Mapson**

ISBN 10: 1-56052-604-1
ISBN 13: 978-1-56052-604-9
Library of Congress Catalog Card Number 00-111979
Printed in the United States of America

8 9 10 09 08

Learning Objectives For:

OFFICE MANAGEMENT

The objectives for *Office Management* are listed below. They have been developed to guide the user to the core issues covered in this book.

THE OBJECTIVES OF THIS BOOK ARE TO HELP THE USER:

1) Understand the role of an office manager

2) Explore the nature of personnel relationships

3) Improve leadership and human relations skills

4) Learn tips about handling special situations

ASSESSING PROGRESS

A Crisp Series **assessment** is available for this book. The 25-item, multiple-choice and true/false questionnaire allows the reader to evaluate his or her comprehension of the subject matter.

To download the assessment and answer key, go to www.courseilt.com and search on the book title.

Assessments should not be used in any employee selection process.

About the Authors

Marilyn Manning, Ph.D., is a certified management consultant, conflict mediator, and international speaker. She facilitates and coaches teams and leaders to solve difficult people problems and organizational challenges. Her interactive keynote speeches and workshops topics include Strategic Planning, Communications, Change and Conflict Management, Teambuilding, and Customer Service. Her clients include University of Chicago, Lucent, GE, Compaq, GTE, US Postal System, National Semiconductor, and Stanford Hospital. To download free business articles, visit www.MManning.com.

Author and consultant Patricia Haddock works with organizations to help people increase productivity and effectiveness. She gives speeches and workshops at association events and conferences and for corporations. She also plans and facilitates meetings and focus groups, and works directly with individuals and teams to improve effectiveness and interpersonal skills. Her clients include the IRS, National Judicial College, and State Compensation Insurance Fund, among others. To have a description of her programs and services mailed or faxed to you, call 888-863-3919. Or visit her website at Speakers.com and Speaking.com.

How to Use This Book

This *Fifty-Minute™ Series Book* is a unique, user-friendly product. As you read through the material, you will quickly experience the interactive nature of the book. There are numerous exercises, real-world case studies, and examples that invite your opinion, as well as checklists, tips, and concise summaries that reinforce your understanding of the concepts presented.

A Crisp *Fifty-Minute™ Book* can be used in variety of ways. Individual self-study is one of the most common. However, many organizations use *Fifty-Minute* books for pre-study before a classroom training session. Other organizations use the books as a part of a system-wide learning program—supported by video and other media based on the content in the books. Still others work with Crisp Learning to customize the material to meet their specific needs and reflect their culture. Regardless of how it is used, we hope you will join the more than 20 million satisfied learners worldwide who have completed a *Fifty-Minute Book*.

Preface

Managing an office is not an easy task. It requires a variety of skills and a lot of patience. For example:

- You must be an effective planner, for both the short and long term.

- You must take appropriate actions to ensure that your plans are met, and be flexible enough to change plans and actions, as necessary.

- You must develop standards and controls that support the goals of your organization.

- You must be a people-person, capable of putting together effective teams to get the job done. You need to know how to hire, train, evaluate, coach, and counsel employees.

- You must lead effectively to get the results you need. This requires you to know how to manage and resolve conflict and negotiate solutions that result in win-win situations for everyone.

- You have to make sure your customers are happy and that their needs are being met.

This book will help you do all of the above. It will teach you new skills or reinforce skills you already have. You will obtain the greatest benefits if you do the exercises in addition to reading the text. This book can also be used as a reference when situations arise that need special attention.

We wish you luck and good managing.

Marilyn Manning, Ph.D.   *Patricia Haddock*

Dedications

To my family: Seth, Melissa, Scott, Uncle Bill, and Michael.
-Marilyn

To my sister, Bev, who always believes.
-Patricia

Contents

Roles and
Responsibilities

"Any business must plan ahead, either to capitalize on success or to reverse the trend if not successful."

–Anonymous

2

What Is Your Role?

Every office needs someone who can manage the three W's so that customers* receive quality service and the business is a success.

Every office needs someone who can manage:

➤ Workers

➤ Workflow

➤ Workplace

That "someone" is the office manager.

That "someone" is YOU.

---

* *Throughout this book, the term* customer *includes* clients.

What Are Your Responsibilities?

As an office manager, you will have many responsibilities and wear many hats. Among the requirements may be:

Planning	Creating a design for future action
Organizing	Identifying and allocating all necessary resources
Decision Making	Researching relevant information and choosing a course of action
Communicating	Giving and receiving feedback
Motivating	Using human relations skills to stimulate employee productivity
Acting	Implementing plans and decisions
Controlling	Measuring performance against plans
Evaluating	Analyzing results versus effort, time, and cost
Leading	Demonstrating by example that the office team is productive, professional, and positive

What Is Your Work Vision?

All good office managers have a vision. Your work vision should:

➤ Dovetail and support your organization's vision and mission

➤ Reflect your ethics and commitment to your organization

You communicate your work vision by stating it simply and understandably. Write it down; publish it for others to see. Tie it into job descriptions, assignments, performance plans, as well as individual and departmental goals. Never let your employees forget the common vision they share.

Take a few minutes to think about your work-related vision and then summarize it in the space below. When you define your vision, think about how it fits in with your vision for the other areas of your life.

My work vision is:

Providing professional and valued support to all colleagues and customers. Ensuring the environment is happy, comfortable and welcoming. Giving and gaining respect from all colleagues, whatever their level

You want to ensure that your work-related vision is aligned with your personal vision. If you discover conflicts, take time to resolve them. Unresolved conflicts between your work and your personal life can lead to stress and poor performance.

Are there conflicts between your work vision and your personal vision? If so, what do you plan to do to resolve them?

Adapted from Leadership Skills for Women _by Marilyn Manning and Patricia Haddock, Crisp Series._

WORK VISION EXERCISE

Defining your values helps you support your vision. List your values below, then think back to your actions during the past month. In the other column, write actions you took that demonstrated your commitment to that value. Refer to your calendar and memos to help you recall actions you took.

Example:

Values I promote on the job:

Open, honest communication

Actions I take:

I completed a written performance evaluation for an employee last week and reviewed it with him. I do this every six months for every employee.

Values I promote on the job:

_____

_____

_____

_____

Actions I take:

_____

_____

_____

_____

_____

_____

_____

If you discovered inconsistencies between your values and your actions, what would you do to resolve them?

_____

_____

Becoming an Effective Planner

One of your primary goals is to satisfactorily fulfill your responsibilities and meet the needs of both customers and employees. This can be accomplished through careful and effective planning. This means you must assess where things stand today, decide where you need to go, formulate goals, and design short- and long-range plans to achieve your objectives and realize your vision.

Steps to Create Your Vision for Your Office

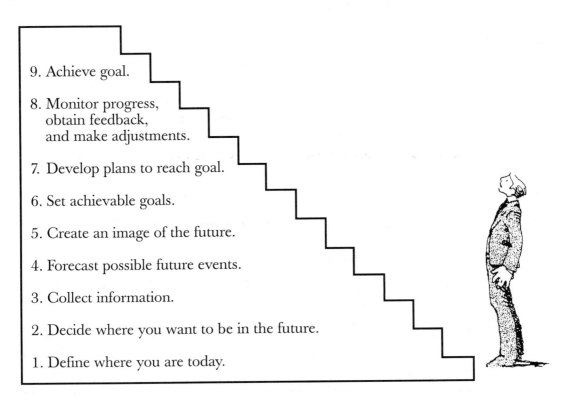

9. Achieve goal.

8. Monitor progress, obtain feedback, and make adjustments.

7. Develop plans to reach goal.

6. Set achievable goals.

5. Create an image of the future.

4. Forecast possible future events.

3. Collect information.

2. Decide where you want to be in the future.

1. Define where you are today.

Planning never stops. Each step of the planning process takes you closer to success.

A System of Plans

As the office manager, you probably will be responsible for developing and implementing operational and project plans and occasionally contributing to strategic plans.

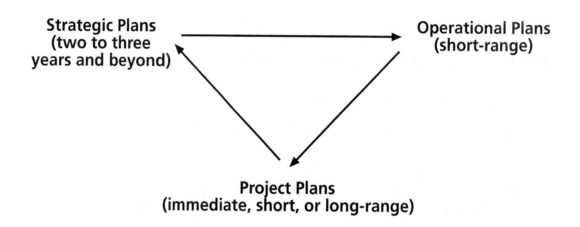

Strategic Plans: Define broad goals and their implementation over the long term. They normally come from the organization's top management.

Operational Plans: Support strategic plans and outline actions to be performed by each functional area.

Project Plans: Support both operational and strategic plans and may include action statements for specific events, such as new product development, office productivity, facilities expansion, installation of new office systems, or reorganization.

Goal Setting

In order to plan effectively, you must be able to establish and reach goals for yourself and your organization.

Goals:

➤ Are statements of results you expect to achieve.

➤ Should be developed with input from all affected parties.

➤ Are specific and measurable.

➤ Describe the criteria you will use to determine if and how well the goals are met.

➤ Usually include a time frame for completion, although some goals may be ongoing, such as goals for employees who perform routine processing functions.

➤ Should be challenging and achievable.

➤ Should be replaced with new goals when the needs of the job change or a specific project is completed.

➤ Must be consistent with office standards.

GOAL SETTING EXERCISE

Write a statement of your company's philosophy or mission statement. Example: "Provide our customers with the highest quality processed photographic prints, at competitive prices, within one hour of drop-off."

_____

_____

Write one short-term goal that supports your mission statement. Example: "Design a new promotional direct market self-mailer or product before the end of the week and stay within budget."

_____

_____

Write one long-term goal that supports your mission statement. Example: "Have all front-line employees attend a three-hour customer service training course before June 1."

_____

_____

Write a personal goal that relates to your job. Example: "Ensure the phone is politely answered before the third ring."

_____

_____

CONTINUED

Write a weekly office goal and your plan to achieve it. Example: "Increase customer contacts by sending out informational product packages to 25 potential new customers each day."

_____

_____

Write a monthly office goal and your plan to achieve it. Example: "Update all computer database files by the end of the month by spending at least one hour each day on this project."

_____

_____

Write a quarterly office goal and your plan to achieve it. Example: "Track sales figures by generating quarterly sales reports and deliver reports to the field within three working days following the end of the quarter."

_____

_____

Write a yearly office goal and your plan to achieve it. Example: "Improve productivity by 15% per employee by constructing and adhering to a yearly budget and by training employees to become more productive."

_____

_____

Keep the Work Flowing

Having good control systems allows you to keep work moving through your office. Once you begin a project, you need a system to make sure it progresses according to your plan toward your goal. Establish controls during the planning process and keep them simple. Then, compare what happens against the control system you have established and revise the goal or process as necessary.

Before a project begins:

- Define the results expected.

- List major steps.

- Set time frames.

- Make schedules.

- Decide what resources you need.

- Set checkpoints.

- Obtain understanding and acceptance from team members.

While the work is being done:

- Require completed reports and updates.

- Follow up at specified checkpoints.

- Monitor the motivation of team members.

After the work is done:

- Evaluate performance and take action to improve performance, as necessary.

- Recognize good work and accomplishments.

For a good book on project management, see Project Management *by Marion E. Haynes, Crisp Series.*

CONTROL SYSTEM
SELF-ASSESSMENT

Some important aspects of control systems are listed below. Indicate your proficiency by checking (✔) the appropriate box.

I normally:

	Do Well	Need to Improve
Establish controls as part of every project.	❑	❑
Set up time schedules and checkpoints to measure progress.	❑	❑
Encourage feedback from team members throughout a project.	❑	❑
Evaluate plans and make adjustments, as necessary.	❑	❑
Adjust objectives, plans, resources, or motivational factors to meet organizational goals.	❑	❑
Communicate progress and plan changes to those who need to know.	❑	❑

What controls do you want to establish?

_____

_____

What controls do you need to improve and how will you improve them?

_____

_____

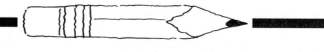

RESPONSIBILITIES WORKSHEET

Making sure that each employee understands his or her responsibility does several things:

➤ Prevents misunderstandings and communication mistakes

➤ Prevents blockages in workflow

List the major activities for which your office has responsibility and the names of employees in charge of those activities. Identify responsibility as primary (**P**) or secondary (**S**).

Activity	Name	Responsibility (P/S)
1. _____	_____	_____
2. _____	_____	_____
3. _____	_____	_____
4. _____	_____	_____
5. _____	_____	_____
6. _____	_____	_____
7. _____	_____	_____
8. _____	_____	_____
9. _____	_____	_____
10. _____	_____	_____

Make sure each employee understands his or her level of responsibility to prevent misunderstandings and blockages in workflow.

Time Management = Productive Work Habits

Another key to keeping the work flowing is to practice effective time management. This begins by examining your own work habits to make sure are being as productive as possible. Are you using your time efficiently? Do your actions support your goals and job requirements? How many of the following do you currently do?

At work, I:

➤ Review my goals daily and link them to my activities for the week.

➤ Set deadlines for all critical activities and meet them.

➤ Plan my schedule for the next day to support my goals.

➤ Schedule creative or challenging activities for my peak hours.

➤ Spend my time doing those things that only I can do.

➤ Use delegation to develop employees' skills and expand their work experience.

➤ Set up paper flow to reduce the possibility of a log jam.

➤ Question assumptions. I don't assume that because I've always done something, I should continue to do it.

➤ Always ask "Is this necessary?" "Is there a faster/easier/better/more efficient way of doing this?"

➤ Lighten up. Laughter releases chemicals that lift spirits and enhance creativity. Look for humor and laugh often.

➤ Do something that supports your personal values every day.

Time Management = Productive Work Habits (continued)

➤ Make requests and give instructions as specifically as possible. Ask others to repeat what they think I said and immediately correct any miscommunication.

➤ Set realistic time frames. Time frames that are too tight can be frustrating; time frames that are too generous contribute to inefficiency.

➤ Avoid ambiguous language. Are my words concrete and specific or vague and obscure? The more precise my word choices, the clearer my communication and the less need for repetition.

Choose six of these work habits to incorporate into your daily routine and circle them.

IDENTIFY TIME WASTERS

Where does your time go? Identify where you waste time and decide how you will eliminate time wasters.

How can I spend less time at meetings?

_____

_____

How can I find files/papers faster?

_____

_____

How can I spend less time on the phone?

_____

_____

How can I save time on business trips?

_____

_____

How can I get people to follow instructions better?

_____

_____

How can I make my work space more efficient?

_____

_____

How can I better prioritize tasks?

_____

_____

Identify Time Wasters (continued)

How can I delegate and know that the work will get done properly?

_____

_____

How can I organize supplies?

_____

_____

How can I get to the bottom of my in-box?

_____

_____

How can I keep track of computer files?

_____

_____

How can I simplify my life?

_____

_____

Are there time wasters not on this list? Write them here:

_____

_____

How will you eliminate the time wasters you have identified?

_____

_____

Watch Out for Time Crime

What happens when employees don't know how to do their jobs, can't do their jobs because something prevents them from doing it, or don't want to do their jobs? They become less productive. They commit "time crime."

Time crime is the disappearance of time at the company's expense. Time crime takes many forms. Do you recognize any of these? Check (✔) those you have experienced:

❑ Extra time tacked on to breaks and/or lunch

❑ Frequent trips to the restroom

❑ Lengthy personal phone calls

❑ Workflow held up by other departments

❑ Inappropriate staffing for the amount of work (too many or too few employees)

❑ Low morale causing negative attitudes and group complaining sessions

❑ Procrastination

If any of these time crimes regularly occur in your office, what steps will you take to eliminate time crime?

_____

_____

Setting Office Guidelines and Procedures

"*Put all your eggs in one basket and watch that basket.*"

–Mark Twain

Effective Guidelines and Procedures for the Office

Every office needs guidelines and procedures that support the organization without imposing unnecessary burdens.

Effective guidelines and procedures:

➤ Are realistic and easily understood

➤ May be developed with input from employees

➤ Should be communicated, understood, and accepted by employees

➤ Should be flexible to allow for revision when business reasons require changes

Some examples of standard office guidelines cover the following:

➤ Required Bulletin Board Notices (federal, state, and local laws)

➤ Office Expense Records and Submission Rules

➤ Dress Code

➤ Attendance

➤ Work Rules

➤ Preventing Sexual Harassment

Required Bulletin Board Notices

Companies must post certain notices as required by federal, state, and local laws and regulations. Check with your legal counselor for state and local posting requirements.

Current Federal Posting Requirements

➤ Minimum Wage

➤ Equal Employment Opportunity is the Law, including:

Age Discrimination in Employment Act

Americans with Disabilities Act

Equal Pay Act

Executive Order 11246 (non-discrimination required by federal contractors)

Rehabilitation Act of 1973

Title VII of 1964 Civil Rights Act

Vietnam Era Veterans Readjustment Assistance Act

➤ Employee Polygraph Protection Act

➤ Family and Medical Leave Act

➤ Job Safety and Health Protection Act

➤ OSHA No. 200 (Annual OSHA summary—posted during February only)

Office Expense Accounts

Every office needs guidelines for office expense accounts. Expenses add to overhead and directly affect the bottom line positively or negatively depending on how well they are monitored and controlled.

Your office should have reimbursement standards to guide employees who incur business-related expenses. Thoughtful controls can add significantly to your organization's financial health.

Here are some recommendations to control expenses:

➤ Require that all expenses be tied to business needs.

➤ Set dollar limits for certain items, such as business lunches, gifts for customers, and non-routine purchases.

➤ Centralize the purchase of supplies, equipment, technology, and travel expenses to take advantage of quantity discounts and maintain consistency throughout the company.

➤ Monitor the use of corporate credit cards.

➤ Require approval for items that exceed a set dollar amount.

Dress Code

Clothing says a great deal about an individual and how employees dress says a great deal about a company. The dress code should reflect the job being performed and the nature of your business.

In a backroom function where employees do not have direct customer contact, a casual dress code may be appropriate. Where employees work directly with customers, clothing should reflect the best possible image. Customer contact employees should dress to make the customer feel comfortable while projecting an image of competence and expertise.

Dress codes can be sensitive subjects for both managers and employees. You may want to develop your dress code with input from employees to provide them with a sense of ownership. In all cases, make sure your employees understand the reasons for the dress code and for any differences that may exist between one function and another.

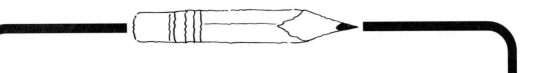

DRESS CODE EXERCISE

To help establish an appropriate dress code for your office, answer these questions.

What kind of image do you want to create, i.e., how do you want others to view your office environment?

_____

_____

What attire would make your customers/clients feel comfortable?

_____

_____

Do you need separate dress codes for different areas of your office?

_____

_____

Are uniforms required for some/all of your employees?

_____

_____

Does your dress code discriminate because of gender?

_____

_____

How does the dress code allow for personal preference?

_____

_____

Attendance

Regular attendance and punctuality are necessary for the efficient running of your office. Employees must report to work as scheduled and work their required hours, including overtime.

In general, an absence is an unscheduled day off, except for days off due to:

➤ Paid vacation and holidays

➤ Leave for bereavement or military duty

➤ Jury duty or time off to vote

➤ Absences covered by laws such as the Family and Medical Leave Act

Make sure all employees complete accurate time records and notify managers before the start of the work day if they cannot come to work or will be late coming to work.

Work Rules

Generally, work rules apply to all employees while they are conducting company business, or while operating company-owned or leased vehicles.

You should make sure that you:

➤ Develop your work rules in conjunction with an attorney to ensure that they comply with applicable laws and regulations.

➤ Clearly communicate work rules to employees.

While it is impossible to provide a complete list of all work rules related to conduct and performance, the following examples are provided to help you decide which should apply to your office.

➤ Using abusive, intimidating language, or inappropriate behavior while on company premises.

➤ Allowing unauthorized passengers in company vehicles or on company property.

➤ Altering or falsifying company records and employment applications.

➤ Acting violently or making threats on company premises.

➤ Insubordination or refusal to perform tasks assigned.

➤ Leaving one's department or company property without approval before the end of a scheduled work shift.

➤ Mishandling, misappropriation, or unauthorized removal or possession of company funds and/or company property.

➤ Possessing, distributing, selling, using, or being under the influence of alcoholic beverages or drugs while working or while on company property.

Work Rules (continued)

➤ Releasing or inappropriately using confidential information about the company or its customers or suppliers.

➤ Sexual harassment or other unlawful harassment of employees or suppliers.

➤ Sleeping while on duty.

➤ Smoking in restricted areas or where "no-smoking" signs are posted.

➤ Unsatisfactory performance or gross negligence.

➤ Violating safety, health, or security rules.

Preventing Sexual Harassment

Title VII of the Civil Rights Act of 1964 prohibits sexual advances, requests for sexual favors, and other verbal or physical conduct of a sexual nature. Sexual harassment can involve charges of intentional infliction of emotional stress, assault and battery, or invasion of the right to privacy. These cases can be filed against the person accused of the harassment as well as the manager of the accused and the company.

Harassment is any behavior of a sexual nature that makes a person uncomfortable, and may include:

➤ Men harassing women

➤ Women harassing men

➤ A person harassing another person of the same sex

If a person's work performance is affected by repeated unwelcome gestures, actions, or language, harassment has taken place. Some actions are considered harassment even if there is only one occurrence.

Preventing Sexual Harassment (continued)

Any of the following situations can be considered sexual harassment:

➤ A person has been made to feel that he/she must submit to or accept sexual overtures as a condition of employment.

➤ A male allows his eyes to wander to a female's anatomy while having a conversation with her.

➤ A person has been made to feel that to submit to or reject sexual advances will affect his/her employment, advancement, evaluation, or work assignment.

➤ A female worker's inappropriate attire causes an uncomfortable distraction among co-workers.

➤ Sexual conduct is intended to, or could possibly, interfere with the individual's work performance.

➤ A person is offended by a dirty joke.

➤ An individual feels sexually intimidated by the work environment.

➤ A supervisor repeatedly invites a subordinate to go out on a date.

➤ Unwanted compliments with sexual overtones are repeated.

➤ A person, making a friendly gesture, pats another in a place that makes the other person uncomfortable.

Adapted from Guide to Affirmative Action *by Pamela J. Conrad and Robert B. Maddux. Thomson Learning.*

Staffing the Office

"*I will pay more for the ability to deal with people than any other ability under the sun.*"

–John D. Rockefeller

34

Key Responsibilities in Staffing

Hiring the right people is vital to your success as an office manager. The person you select should be evaluated carefully against an updated written job description to insure he or she has the skills and experience to satisfactorily fulfill the job requirements. The ultimate success of your organization is related to the quality of your hiring decisions.

Follow the six steps listed below to help you clarify your hiring decision:

Step 1 Review the job description to ensure it is current.

Step 2 Involve key staff people to ensure the job description reflects what the job requires. Rewrite the job description based on input.

Step 3 Prepare a list of specific legal questions to ask the candidates.

Step 4 Record interview responses on a rating form.

Step 5 Determine the best candidate by reviewing assessments made on the rating form.

Step 6 Make a job offer.

EEO Guidelines for Office Managers

You must protect the rights of your employees and your company under current federal Equal Employment Opportunity (EEO) legislation. You must recruit, select, employ, transfer, and promote employees and administer all compensation and employee benefit programs based on individual qualifications and performance, without regard to race, religion, sex, national origin, age, color, physical or mental disability (or perceived disability), Vietnam Era or disabled Veteran status. States and local governments may have additional EEO requirements. See legal counsel for information about your area.

The following guidelines suggest a positive way to comply with EEO requirements.

➤ EEO legislation is complex and is constantly being tested and interpreted in the courts. Be alert for changes. When in doubt about how to proceed, seek the advice of your legal counsel.

➤ Create and maintain an atmosphere within your organization that demonstrates you are aware of EEO policies and support them.

➤ Refuse to permit discriminatory acts of any type by anyone in your office. Racial slurs, jokes, and sexual harassment are offensive and have no place on the job. Even seemingly small incidents can make people uncomfortable and lead to charges of discrimination and subsequent investigations.

➤ Analyze the positions you manage to ensure the qualifications required of the people who fill them are based on bona fide job requirements.

➤ Be sure non-discriminatory practices are being followed in all recruitment and hiring activities.

➤ Look for possible inequities in pay, job assignments, special projects, training, and promotional practices in your jurisdiction and correct them.

➤ Make an effort to support and assist qualified females, minorities, and handicapped persons to advance within your company.

➤ Document any disciplinary action you take and reasons for selection, termination, transfer, promotion, or other personnel action. Be sure your documentation is adequate to support the action. If there is any doubt, check with legal counsel.

➤ Do not retain unsatisfactory performers for any reason. Make every reasonable effort to help them meet standards and document these efforts. If an employee cannot do the job, terminate him/her or move them to a position they can do adequately.

Adapted from Guide to Affirmative Action *by Pamela J. Conrad and Robert B. Maddux, Crisp Series.*

AVOIDING ILLEGAL EMPLOYMENT PRACTICES

The following practices reflect the thrust of current legislation and the dangers inherent in careless personnel practices and techniques. Check (✔) those you need to learn more about and make sure you get the assistance you need.

Under current legislation, it is unlawful to:

❏ Show a bias in help-wanted advertising for or against applicants based on any factor covered by EEO legislation.

❏ Use any screening techniques for employment or promotion, i.e., paper and pencil tests, questionnaires, etc., that cannot be proved to be directly job-related.

❏ Categorize job candidates on the basis of factors covered by EEO legislation.

❏ Condone or permit harassment, including sexual harassment, of employees.

❏ Segregate employees by race, religion, or national origin with respect to working areas, toilet, locker, and/or recreational facilities.

❏ Cause or attempt to cause an employer to discriminate against any person because of factors covered by EEO legislation through actions initiated by a union.

❏ Refuse to hire a woman because separate facilities would have to be provided.

❏ Perpetuate past discriminatory practices that have led to statistical imbalances in the workplace.

❏ Discharge, lay off, or otherwise terminate an employee on the basis of factors covered by EEO legislation.

Promoting Diversity to Improve Morale and Productivity

People want to feel that they are important and that their contribution matters. Recognizing and using people's abilities and experiences involves them in a way that builds rapport, respect, ownership, and loyalty. The higher morale is, the harder employees are likely to work—the result is increased productivity.

Businesses receive many benefits by recognizing and encouraging workforce diversity. Among the many benefits, consider the economic impact of these top three:

1. Tapping into tremendous purchasing power.

- Older Americans spend more than $800 billion annually

- Minority markets buy more goods and services than any country that trades with the US

- Understanding different values and perspectives opens new markets

2. Reducing costs by reducing employee turnover.

- Highly trained workers will stay with companies that are responsive to their needs

- Retraining is expensive

- High employee turnover reduces morale and productivity

3. Receiving the benefits of productivity, creativity, and innovation from all employees.

- New perspectives enhance problem solving

- Business success is often dependent on group performance

- An inclusive environment builds respect, ownership, and loyalty

Adapted from Dynamics of Diversity: Strategic Programs for Your Organization *by Odette Pollar and Rafael Gonzales, Crisp Series.*

Writing Job Descriptions

A professionally developed job description includes the following five elements:

1. The purpose of the job.

- What product or service is supported by the job?

- How does the job relate to other jobs in the office?

- What is the result of poor or non-performance?

2. What the employee does on the job.

- What are the most important job duties?

- How often are they performed?

- What kind of decisions is the person responsible for making?

3. How is the job performed?

- What are reporting relationships?

- What contacts are required inside the company?

- What contacts are required outside the company?

- What are the working conditions?

4. What human relations or personal skills are needed?

- What interpersonal skills are needed?

- Does the position require detail orientation, logic, mathematical, reasoning, or writing skills?

- What skills are absolutely essential?

- What kind of grooming is required?

5. What physical qualities are necessary?

- Is physical strength required?

- Is size a factor?

Adapted from Quality Interviewing *by Robert B. Maddux, Crisp Series.*

Interviewing Potential Employees

After you have developed your job description, you are ready to evaluate candidates against the criteria you have set.

Follow these tips for effective interviews.

➤ Use phone interviews to obtain information and screen candidates.

➤ Decide what parts of the resume are most important for the open position.

➤ Learn about the candidate's previous job experience before offering an opportunity to interview for your open position.

➤ Hold the interview in a place where you won't be disturbed or interrupted.

➤ Establish a relaxed rapport early. Put the candidate at ease.

➤ Use open-ended questions that require more than "yes" or "no" answers. Some open-ended questions are "What are your best skills for this job?" and "What was your most significant achievement on your last job?"

➤ Use some self-appraisal questions that require candidates to display reasoning and/or problem-solving skills.

➤ Set up hypothetical situations that require the candidate to display reasoning and/or problem-solving skills.

➤ Thoroughly explore the candidate's experience and education relative to job requirements.

➤ Use active listening techniques and repeat key items the candidate says.

➤ Take notes on paper other than the application or resume. Keep in mind that all notes can be subpoenaed in a legal action.

Interviewing Potential Employees (continued)

➤ Evaluate all candidates using the same criteria.

➤ Request additional interviews with the most likely candidates and other key personnel.

➤ Thoroughly check references.

➤ Make a written offer of employment for the most likely candidate.

During the interview, be prepared to discuss the following information about the job and the company:

➤ A history of the company, including key products and services.

➤ The company's vision and mission.

➤ The job description that explains duties and responsibilities.

➤ How and when performance will be evaluated.

➤ Work hours, rules, and other information about the office.

➤ Compensation and benefits information.

Good Job Interview Questions

Ask questions that will uncover job-related skills only. Questions on factors covered by EEO legislation are prohibited. Write out some specific questions for a position you plan to fill using the criteria described earlier.

Experience and Education

Example: "Describe a typical day in your current job."

_____

_____

Intelligence and Aptitude

Example: "How do you make decisions? What process do you use?"

_____

_____

Attitudes and Personality

Example: "What has frustrated you most in your business life?"

_____

_____

Job Skills and Knowledge

Example: "What strengths would you bring to this job?"

_____

_____

CANDIDATE DISPOSITION FORM

You may be required to show that you evaluated all candidates for a position on the same basis. You must be able to demonstrate the criteria you used in making your hiring decision were job-related. Keep carefully written documentation to avoid possible lawsuits.

The following reasons for rejecting a candidate are valid as long as they don't apply to the person chosen for the job.

Candidate:

___ Does not meet minimum job requirements.

___ Meets minimum job requirements, but is not the best qualified.

___ Has no prior related experience.

___ Has less prior experience than the person selected.

___ Has a lower level of skills than the person selected.

___ Has less directly-related training than the person selected.

___ Cannot work the schedule required by the job.

___ Withdrew self from consideration.

Comments: _____

_____

Candidate name: _____

Date:_____

Position applied for:_____

Job offer will ❏ will not ❏ be extended.

Job-related reason(s) candidate selected was best qualified:

_____

_____

Adapted from Quality Interviewing *by Robert B. Maddux, Crisp Series.*

Effective Employee Orientation

Thoughtful employee orientation is another important activity you will perform as an office manager. An employee's first few days on the job are critical to the employee's success. Often, an employee's attitude about the organization he or she will be working for is set on that crucial first day.

Your orientation program should include the following:

- ❏ A sincere welcome

- ❏ An introduction to key people in the office

- ❏ A tour of the office and building, including emergency exits

- ❏ A description of the fundamentals, such as office hours and rules, benefits, emergency procedures, safety, attendance policy, etc.

- ❏ A description of job duties and minimum job requirements

- ❏ A description of initial training the employee will receive

- ❏ Time for the employee to familiarize him/herself with the work area

- ❏ A fully-equipped desk or work space

- ❏ Documents, such as benefits handbook, company phone directory, etc.

- ❏ A first assignment

Steps for On-the-Job Training

Every training program has four steps:

Step 1: Define how the job should be done

Step 2: Plan the training

Step 3: Present the training

Step 4: Evaluate the training

On-the-job training is popular in small offices and companies. Many office managers believe that it is one of the most effective forms of training. But on-the-job training only works if you plan it carefully.

The following should be part of your on-the-job training program.

➤ Task lists, performance standards, and training plans and lessons for each task

➤ Trainers who want to train and who understand basic training principles

➤ Written materials, such as manuals and workbooks to reinforce what is taught

➤ Enough time to train properly

➤ Necessary tools and supplies to do an effective training job

➤ A means of evaluating the training

If any of the above are missing from your on-the-job training programs, write action plans below to incorporate them into your training procedures.

_____

_____

_____

_____

Adapted from Training Managers to Train *by Herman E. Zaccarelli, Crisp Series.*

Coaching and Counseling

Effective managers know how to coach and how to counsel employees. Even more important, they understand the differences between these skills and when to use each. The following are brief definitions.

Counseling: A *supportive* process by a manager to help an employee define and work through personal problems that affect job performance.

Coaching: A *directive* process by a manager to train and orient an employee to the realities of the workplace and to help the employee remove barriers to optimum work performance.

Counseling and coaching share many of the same skills. At times they may seem to overlap. When they do, remember the following diagrams. They will help you differentiate these two processes.

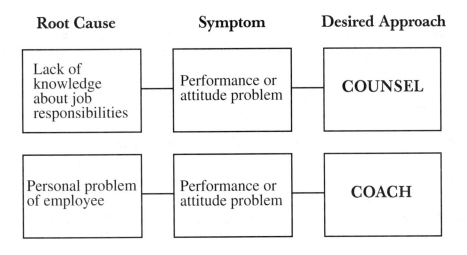

Root Cause	Symptom	Desired Approach
Lack of knowledge about job responsibilities	Performance or attitude problem	**COUNSEL**
Personal problem of employee	Performance or attitude problem	**COACH**

Information on coaching and counseling skills was adapted from Marianne Minor's book Coaching and Counseling, *Crisp Series.*

THE BENEFITS OF COACHING AND COUNSELING

Review the list of benefits below and check (✔) those which will help you improve your current workplace challenges.

- ❏ Makes your job easier when employees build their skill levels.

- ❏ Enables greater delegation so you can have more time to truly manage versus "do for."

- ❏ Builds your reputation as a "people developer."

- ❏ Increases productivity when employees know what the goals are and how to achieve them.

- ❏ Develops sharing of leadership responsibilities.

- ❏ Increases employee motivation and initiative through positive recognition and feedback.

- ❏ Increases likelihood of tasks being completed in a quality way.

- ❏ Avoids surprises and defensiveness in performance appraisals.

- ❏ Increases creativity and innovation of unit as employees feel safe to take risks.

- ❏ Increases team cohesiveness due to clarified goals and roles.

Improving Productivity

To improve office productivity, you have to get employees excited about their work and accomplishments. Every employee wants to feel satisfied about his or her contributions. Satisfaction relates to five basic needs defined by psychologist Abraham Maslow, who observed that each person has the same basic needs and spends each day satisfying one or more of them. Maslow's hierarchy of needs are:

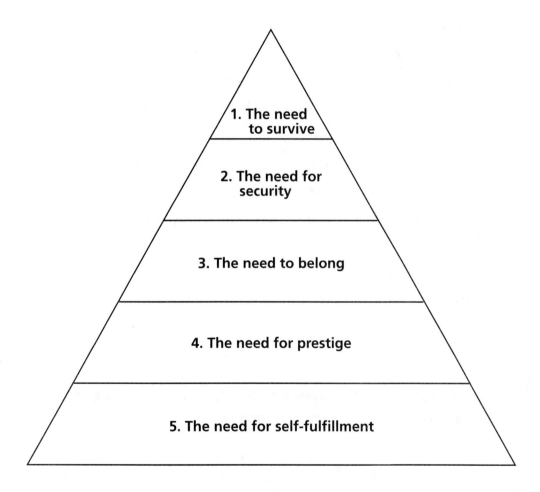

1. The need to survive

2. The need for security

3. The need to belong

4. The need for prestige

5. The need for self-fulfillment

How Productive Are You?

Rate yourself on how effectively you meet your employees' needs. Rate how well you perform the following activities using this scale:

5 = highest 1 = not at all

___ I am an efficient manager.

___ I encourage and teach employees to think for themselves.

___ I arrange work so employees can see the end result.

___ I assign work to make it as interesting as possible to everyone.

___ I listen to ideas on how to do things better.

___ I inform those who need to know about what is going on.

___ I treat employees like professionals at all times.

___ I recognize individuals and teams for good work, both formally and informally.

___ I offer challenges whenever possible.

___ I encourage staff development.

___ **TOTAL**

A score of 24 to 30 means you are an outstanding office manager and your office work flow is probably very productive. Fifteen to 23 means you have potential, but can improve how you motivate employees to produce. Eight to 14 indicates that you understand the principles, but you aren't applying them to your office. You may want to enroll in a management class. A score of zero to seven may indicate that you need extensive training in order to improve productivity.

Evaluating Employee Performance

The performance goals you establish define two things:

➤ What you want done

➤ How you want it done

The performance appraisal process evaluates how well each employee has met these goals, based on criteria established.

Performance appraisals have three basic functions:

1. To provide adequate feedback to each employee on his or her performance.

2. To serve as an opportunity to discuss, face-to-face, any adjustments or changes to existing performance objectives.

3. To provide data to managers or supervisors so they can evaluate an employee, job assignments, and compensation.

Formal performance appraisals should be conducted:

➤ On a regular basis that is established in writing

➤ At a pre-determined time and place, free of interruptions

➤ Using a document upon which performance can be summarized in writing

➤ Separately from the compensation review

➤ With a written follow-up outlining any action plans resulting from the performance session

WHAT CAN WELL-PLANNED PERFORMANCE APPRAISALS DO FOR YOU?

Performance appraisals often take a low priority on an office manager's schedule. However, the appraisal process is an essential communication between you and your employees and shouldn't be ignored. There are several advantages in doing appraisals in a timely and professional manner. Check (✔) those that you agree are important:

❑ Performance appraisals provide valuable insights into the work the employee is doing and how it is being done.

❑ When you maintain good communication with employees about job expectations and results, you create opportunities for new ideas and improved methods.

❑ When you give well-planned, timely performance appraisals, employees know how they are doing and that knowledge reduces their uncertainty.

❑ When employees receive timely corrective feedback, productivity is improved.

❑ Appraisals provide an opportunity to reinforce sound work habits and publicly recognize good performance.

❑ Appraisals encourage two-way communication.

❑ Learning to write and give good performance appraisals is excellent preparation for advancement and increased responsibility.

Adapted from Performance Management *by Robert B. Maddux, Crisp Series.*

Eight Steps for More Effective Performance Appraisals

Step 1 When an employee is hired or assigned to your office, provide a written description of the behaviors and qualities required for the job.

Step 2 Set specific goals with the employee and put your agreement in writing.

Step 3 Make sure the goals are fair and reasonable so they allow you to evaluate how well the employee is doing.

Step 4 Explain that the performance review process is designed to evaluate how well goals are met and the means by which the employee achieved them.

Step 5 Obtain agreement with the employee about which behaviors and performance criteria will be achieved.

Step 6 Set a date for the first review. Make sure you schedule the first review within any probationary period required by your office.

Step 7 Observe the employee during the review period and document incidents of behavior that affect the employee's performance or illustrate behavior patterns.

Step 8 Schedule the actual appraisal far enough in advance to allow the employee to prepare.

Appraisal Pitfalls to Avoid

An appraiser must be on guard against anything that distorts reality—favorably or unfavorably. If you are responsible for performance evaluations, remember: Concentrate on performance measured against mutually understood expectations.

Some typical pitfalls include:

➤ Bias/Prejudice: Things we tend to react to that have nothing to do with performance such as sex, race, religion, education, family background, age, etc.

➤ Trait Assessment: Too much attention to characteristics that have nothing to do with the job and are difficult to measure. Examples include characteristics such as flexibility, sincerity, and friendliness.

➤ Over-emphasis on favorable or unfavorable performance of one or two tasks that could lead to an unbalanced evaluation of the overall contribution.

➤ Relying on impressions rather than facts.

➤ Holding the employee responsible for the impact of factors beyond his/her control.

➤ Failure to provide each employee with an opportunity for advance preparation.

Adapted from Performance Management *by Robert B. Maddux, Crisp Series.*

Discussing Unsatisfactory Performance

Employees who work in a non-threatening atmosphere are more likely to discuss their shortcomings in the appraisal setting. When this occurs, the manager can be supportive by saying something like, "That's very perceptive. What can we do to correct this situation?"

If the employee's performance has been unsatisfactory in an aspect of his or her job, and does not bring up areas of weak performance, the manager must do so. It will benefit both you and the employee to describe the impact of poor performance on the organization.

Some employees may not realize they are falling short of expectations. Or they may assume everything is acceptable because no one has ever discussed the problem with them. Sometimes, they may feel everything is okay because they see others doing the same thing.

Before you attempt to correct unsatisfactory performance, you must first review expectations with the employee. If the employee is unaware of these expectations, they must be made clear and a commitment made that they will be met. If expectations are not being met for some other reason, the manager must first learn why, and then agree on a corrective action plan worked out with the employee.

Questions like these can be helpful in opening up the issues:

"Are you aware of the standards for quantity and quality we expect on this item?"

"Are you aware of your error rate versus the departmental average?"

"We seem to be running about two weeks behind schedule. Can you tell me why and what we can do to catch up?"

"Your sales reports are excellent but they are seldom on time. Can you explain why?"

"Fifty percent of your staff resigned in the last quarter. To what do you attribute that?"

Adapted from Performance Management *by Robert B. Maddux, Crisp Series.*

Handling Poor Performance

You must follow a specific procedure for handling poor performers. In addition to being a sound management practice, there are legal considerations as well. The following steps need to be taken when an employee's performance is not satisfactory.

Step 1: Coaching

Coaching occurs when you work with an employee to remove barriers to optimum work performance. This should occur after you review expectations with the employee. You use coaching when an employee has a performance or attitude problem, or shows a lack of knowledge about job responsibilities.

Step 2: Verbal Notice

Verbal notice can be part of the coaching process. It requires you to say to the employee, "Unless your attitude and/or performance improves, you will be placed on probation." It is essential for you to provide specifics so the employee understands precisely what his or her problems are.

Step 3: Written Notice

Written notice normally follows the verbal notice. Both you and the employee must sign the written notice and place it in the employee's file. It should tell the employee specifically what he or she must do to avoid being placed on probation. It must also tell the employee by what date corrective action must be demonstrated.

Step 4: Probation

This is a formal notification that the employee is on probation and failure to correct behaviors or performance within a specified time frame will result in termination. Make sure this step is performed in conjunction with your human resources department.

Step 5: Termination

The human resources department or your attorney should review the situation with your documentation before you can terminate an employee. Never fire an employee on the spot or without ensuring the termination action is fully documented.

Terminating Employees

When you make hiring decisions, there should be a good fit between the job and the employee. But even the best interviewers hire people who don't work out. Here are some reasons why that happens.

Why things go wrong:

- A candidate was able to mask or defuse certain problems by being an adept interviewee.

- The employee experienced changes in personal or professional goals while on the job that affected his or her fit with the job.

- Situation considerations such as bad chemistry between co-workers or changing responsibilities did not meet with an employee's expectations.

List other reasons why an employee may not work out:

- _____
- _____
- _____

GUIDELINES FOR TERMINATING EMPLOYEES

1. Focus only on the relevant job behaviors and documented performance measurements when conducting the final termination interview.

2. Offer some constructive comments, but be sure that they do not imply you would rehire the person or rescind the termination.

3. Conduct the termination interview in a quiet, private place where you will not be interrupted.

4. Terminate the employee early in the week so there can be some adjustment to the reality by the weekend.

5. Document everything.

6. Before the termination interview, work with your human resources department or company attorney. Make sure you are clear about the provisions of the termination. Is the employee to pack up and leave that day? Can she or her stay for a period of days? Will there be any outplacement help offered? What are the provisions for benefit continuation and for what periods of time?

7. Make sure all of the above is in writing and given to the employee to review and sign.

8. At the time of termination, get any necessary releases from legal action or any agreement about non-disclosure that may be required.

9. Make sure you have the employee's final paycheck on his/her last day of employment.

10. Have the employee return all company credit cards, equipment such as cell phones or computers, software, etc.

11. Change all entry codes and passwords of which the employee had knowledge.

Your Leadership

Effectiveness

"*No member of a crew is praised for the rugged
individuality of his rowing.*"

–Ralph Waldo Emerson

Communicating for Results

Effective communication is critically important in an office. When you have strong communication skills, you are much more effective than colleagues without those skills. Good communicators know what to say and how to say it, either verbally or written, whether in a small office meeting, or in front of a large audience.

Effective communication skills will:

- ➤ Increase confidence, credibility, and competence

- ➤ Reduce misunderstandings and confusion

- ➤ Save time for everyone

- ➤ Help you better negotiate your positions on project and budget matters

Developing effective oral and written communication skills is essential for anyone in a managerial job. Those same skills are equally valuable at home, in volunteer organizations, and memberships in professional associations

When you know how to communicate effectively, you are able to:

- ➤ Influence through your ideas and opinions

- ➤ Listen for and accurately repeat what others say

- ➤ Choose the correct words, timing, and body language for your listener

Listening Actively

Active listening is demonstrating empathy for the speaker, setting aside judgments, listening for facts, emotions, needs, and intent. It is showing understanding and interest.

1. Listen to facts, ideas, and intent.

2. Visually observe and assess the speaker's non-verbal communication. Interpret what the speaker is "saying" with body language, such as eye contact, tone of voice, facial expression, and posture.

3. Monitor your own non-verbal communication. Be aware of the messages you are sending with your body language.

4. Notice your emotional triggers and their effect on you.

5. Try to put yourself in the speaker's shoes. Identify what motivates him or her.

6. Harmonize with the speaker's stress (pain/emotions). Use empathy to absorb the tension.

HOW WELL DO YOU LISTEN?

Think about your communication habits. Below you will find examples of conversations. Rate yourself on a scale from one to five (five being the highest) on how well you listen.

___ A dialog with someone who has a problem

___ A conversation with someone who is passing on information

___ A group problem solving session

___ A casual talk

Consider one of the situations above, for which you rated yourself less than five and complete the following questions. Check (✔) any that apply.

Did you...

❑ Interrupt?

❑ Show impatience as you waited for the person to finish?

❑ Suggest solutions before the situation was fully explained?

❑ Demonstrate through body language (rolling eyes, etc.) that you were not interested?

❑ Spend more time talking than listening?

❑ Think about what you would say next rather than listening?

LISTENING QUIZ

What are your attitudes about listening? To find out, answer the following questions.

	Yes	Seldom
1. I listen between the lines.	❏	❏
2. I listen carefully for all ideas.	❏	❏
3. I take notes during meetings.	❏	❏
4. I wait to hear the entire message before evaluating it.	❏	❏
5. I do not get distracted easily.	❏	❏
6. I listen without letting my emotions show.	❏	❏
7. I respond with appropriate body language.	❏	❏
8. I keep distractions to a minimum.	❏	❏
9. I acknowledge my biases and listen openly.	❏	❏
10. I refrain from interrupting.	❏	❏
11. I keep good eye contact.	❏	❏
12. I often restate or paraphrase to assure understanding.	❏	❏
13. I listen for emotional meaning.	❏	❏
14. I ask questions for clarification.	❏	❏
15. I don't finish the other person's thought or sentence.	❏	❏
16. I concentrate.	❏	❏

Total Score: (yes) _____ (seldom) _____

Count up the number of "seldom" response you checked.
1-4 "seldom" answers: You're applying excellent listening skills.
5-8 "seldom" answers: You're doing well but could improve some areas.
9-12 "seldom" answers: Practice helps; try applying new listening skills.
13-16 "seldom" answers: You could use coaching or listening instruction.

Adapted from The Business of Listening *by Diana Bonet, Crisp Series.*

Listening Tips

A good listener is able to reduce mistakes and misunderstandings.

The following tips will help improve your listening skills:

1. Learn to pause when talking.

2. Imagine the other person's viewpoint. Picture yourself in her position: doing her work, facing her problems, using her language, having her values.

3. Look, act, and be interested. Don't read your mail, doodle, or shuffle.

4. Observe non-verbal behavior.

5. Don't interrupt.

6. Listen between the lines and look for omissions.

7. Speak only affirmatively while listening. Avoid evaluative or critical comments.

8. Rephrase to clarify.

9. Stop talking. Practice attentive silence.

Communication Tips

Here are some quick tips that will help you better plan, deliver, and listen when you are communicating with others.

When listening:

➤ Pay attention to what others say as they say it. Don't think of your response. Just listen.

➤ Express interest by nodding, making appropriate eye contact, and smiling.

When planning to communicate:

➤ Concentrate on no more than three major points. This is the most that a person can absorb in a single communication.

➤ Communicate technical information by starting with simple ideas and moving to more complex ones.

➤ Create images by using stories and real-life examples that people can relate to.

➤ Use stories sparingly and appropriately to help people understand how things apply to them.

➤ Know your subject so well you can field 95% of the questions you might be asked.

➤ Plan the points you want to make and create arguments to refute challenges before you need them.

➤ Ask for what you want and if you hear "No," start negotiating.

➤ Make sure your communication tells people how to save time or money, be healthier, wealthier, wiser, more popular, in control, important, safer, happier, or sexier. In other words, give benefits.

➤ Mentally rehearse a communication by visualizing it exactly as you want it to go. The subconscious doesn't know the difference between reality and imagination. Practice how you will respond to different comments or confrontation. Every time you visualize the communication, it is as if you have performed it.

When communicating in writing:

➤ Make sure each paragraph develops only one idea.

➤ Avoid passive voice. Look for every use of the verb "to be" and rewrite the sentence in active voice.

➤ Vary sentence length to create variety.

➤ Proofread everything before sending it—especially email messages.

➤ Never mail or publish anything that hasn't been spell-checked by your computer.

➤ Let written communications sit for at least a day before you send them out. Time will help reveal mistakes you won't see right away.

When communicating in-person:

➤ Modulate your voice to create emphasis and interest.

➤ Read body language to find out if you're getting your message across.

➤ Ask open-ended questions that require more than simple "Yes" or "No" answers.

➤ Paraphrase what the other person says and ask if you are interpreting their comments correctly.

➤ Relate a new idea to something your audience already knows. For example, the empty space in an atom is proportionally equal to the empty space between planets in our solar system.

Communication Tips (continued)

➤ Use silence to draw out a response from a reluctant speaker.

➤ Require straightforward answers to your questions. Repeat your question until the person responds appropriately.

➤ Make sure everything you say serves you.

➤ Eliminate fillers such as "ummm" and "uhhhh" from your speech to gain more power.

➤ The words "but" and "however" weaken your authority.

➤ Speak from your diaphragm and the back of your throat to project authority.

➤ Always give people something of value to take away with them.

➤ Keep every communication as simple as possible.

➤ Eliminate anything that doesn't contribute to the point you are making.

➤ Always use simple words.

➤ Make sure your body language matches what you are saying to enhance credibility and create congruence.

➤ Use appropriate arm and hand movements to create emphasis. Do not touch people.

➤ In one-on-one communication, look at the other person's forehead, not directly into the eyes, to make comfortable, non-confrontational eye contact.

➤ Stand and sit upright with both feet firmly on the ground to communicate authority and expertise.

➤ Move purposefully, not randomly.

➤ Smile when you communicate in person or on the phone.

➤ Stand while on the phone to energize your speaking.

➤ Lean toward people to express enthusiasm.

➤ Shake hands firmly and enthusiastically.

➤ Don't cross your arms or clasp your hands.

➤ Avoid jargon. Never assume people understand insider terms.

➤ Improve your vocabulary by reading; improve your speaking by listening.

➤ If you feel nervous, take long, slow, deep breaths and firmly plant both feet on the floor.

➤ Use more nouns and verbs than adjectives and adverbs to power-up your communication skills.

➤ If you want questions, ask for them. When asked a question, repeat the question to make sure you understand what is being asked, then, answer.

Giving and Receiving Feedback

Feedback is a means to either reinforce positive behaviors or to ask for modifications of negative behaviors. For example, if you want your assistant to keep proofreading carefully, give him praise when he does so, such as: "I really appreciated your attention to detail in this report."

On the other hand, feedback can be a way to let someone know that their behavior has had a negative impact. If you have a co-worker who is constantly late to work, try this: "I noticed you were late 10 minutes on Monday and 15 minutes today. When you are late, I miss some deadlines, since I need your input to complete certain tasks. How can we better coordinate our time?"

Feedback should be conducted diplomatically. It should be specific and meaningful. Make your words meaningful and specific when giving feedback. Choose the best words to let your listener know how his or her behavior or actions impacted you. Select the best environment in which to communicate. Make sure the timing is right and, as much as possible, eliminate distractions. Know what you want to say, why you want to say it, and what results you want to achieve. Present your points in a calm, clear, and rational way.

Steps when giving feedback:

1. Describe the behavior.

2. Provide firsthand information based on your observations and actions.

3. State specific details, citing recent examples.

4. Focus on changeable behavior and information likely to benefit the receiver.

5. Describe the impact on you and the desired change.

6. Use "I" not "you" statements. Avoid critical or evaluative statements.

7. Use positive body language and reassurance.

Guidelines for receiving feedback:

Whenever you give feedback, remember: Be prepared to listen and receive. Use these guidelines for receiving feedback:

➤ Keep an open mind; be willing to hear ways to improve.

➤ Listen without interrupting, justifying, or explaining.

➤ Paraphrase the feedback so that the person who gave it can determine if you understood the intended message.

➤ If you do not understand, ask for an example for further explanation.

Making the Most of Phone Conversations

Your voice is your most important tool when you are on the phone. You don't have the use of your facial expressions or gestures to help you get your message across. Here are do's and don'ts for making the most of every phone call.

Do

➤ Speak clearly and enunciate every word precisely.

➤ Speak slower than you would if you were meeting in person since it takes people longer to process auditory messages.

➤ Keep your greeting brief. Identify yourself and your reason for calling.

➤ Ask the person if this is a good time to talk.

➤ Plan what you want to accomplish with the call.

➤ Leave a message that states times when you can be reached by phone.

➤ Always leave your phone number. Don't make the other person look it up.

➤ Sound friendly and professional.

➤ Make friends with administrative assistants and receptionists.

➤ Ask permission before putting someone on hold and explain why it is necessary. Thank them when you return to the phone.

➤ Focus your attention on the other person.

Do Not

➤ Record, long, cutesy voicemail messages or greetings that sound unprofessional.

➤ Put people on hold for more than two minutes without giving them an update.

➤ Carry on side conversations while you are on the phone.

➤ Allow interruptions while you are on the phone.

➤ Type on your computer keyboard.

➤ Read your email.

➤ Deliver a canned greeting.

➤ Persist if the person gives you a firm "No."

➤ Play telephone tag.

➤ Speed up when you leave your phone number.

➤ Leave rambling messages.

➤ Vent on voicemail since recorded messages can be forwarded to others and come back to haunt you.

➤ Leave very personal or confidential information on voicemail.

➤ Chew gum or eat while talking on the phone.

Building Successful Teams

Effective managers are team leaders, pulling employees together to meet common goals. Office managers are often responsible for creating and leading teams. Teams need to understand what their goals are and who is responsible to ensure they are met. Keeping your team informed is one of your most important responsibilities as a team leader. You must also identify players outside of the team and coordinate how your team works with them.

Planning is the key that makes teams effective and productive. Good planning eliminates confusion and duplication of effort. Without careful planning, time, effort, and money are often wasted.

Seven rules for team leaders:

Rule 1: Make sure goals are clearly communicated and understood.

Rule 2: Provide opportunities to meet and exchange ideas with team members.

Rule 3: Treat employees with equal respect and give each an opportunity to make a personal contribution to the outcome.

Rule 4: Set a good example by supporting company policies and procedures.

Rule 5: Act consistently and positively. Walk your talk.

Rule 6: Stay calm under pressure.

Rule 7: Keep all promises made to team members.

Identify three ways you can begin to apply these rules immediately, write them in the space provided below:

_____

_____

Adapted from Leadership Skills for Women *by Marilyn Manning and Patricia Haddock, Crisp Series.*

TEAM PLANNING EXERCISE

An effective manager doesn't work alone. What is your team planning proficiency?

I regularly

	Do well	Could Improve
Interpret team goals passed down from upper management.	❏	❏
Convert the needs of the organization into goals and objectives for my team.	❏	❏
Evaluate options and select actions that contribute to reaching goals.	❏	❏
Determine resources needed to meet goals, including people, money, materials, facilities, etc.	❏	❏
Establish deadlines and timelines for all goals.	❏	❏
Set performance standards and measurements for establishing goals and evaluating progress.	❏	❏

TEAM LEADERSHIP ACTION PLAN

The following checklist will help you identify ways to improve your skills as a team leader. Read the list and check (✔) those which are applicable:

I do the following:

	Often	Sometimes	Seldom
I work to develop the skills of others.	❏	❏	❏
I use time efficiently.	❏	❏	❏
I am well organized.	❏	❏	❏
I have good listening skills.	❏	❏	❏
I openly express my views.	❏	❏	❏
I encourage others to express their views.	❏	❏	❏
I maintain open communication in the team.	❏	❏	❏
I deal constructively with conflict.	❏	❏	❏
I share objectives with my team and other teams.	❏	❏	❏
I identify mutual needs and goals.	❏	❏	❏
I support team members' growth and achievement.	❏	❏	❏
I negotiate well.	❏	❏	❏

Any of the above for which you checked "sometimes" or "seldom" are areas you should focus on in your development plan.

Conducting Effective Meetings

Most of us spend a great deal of time in meetings. Recall the last meeting you led or attended. Was it the best use of everyone's time? Instead of wasting time in meetings, learn to use your team meetings to motivate and be creative.

Focus on the key elements of the meeting:

➤ Define the outcome: What, specifically, do you want to accomplish?

➤ Create and distribute a meeting agenda that includes all of the following information:

- Date, time, and location of the meeting
- Meeting objectives
- Discussion items, time frames, and discussion objectives

➤ Agree on ground rules.

➤ Define meeting roles: Who will facilitate? Keep time? Record?

➤ Redistribute the agenda at the start of the meeting and review it with participants.

Before the meeting:

➤ Is the time invested worth the cost? Are key people able to attend?

➤ Have participants adequately prepared for the meeting?

➤ Have you clearly stated your objectives and written the agenda?

➤ Have you checked logistics, room, handouts, equipment needs?

Decision Making and Leadership

Most decisions involve an element of risk or uncertainty. No matter how much information you have, you cannot absolutely guarantee the outcome. Good leaders are good decision makers even when it means taking a risk.

The following tips will help you develop your decision-making skills.

To become a more effective leader:

> **Define the situation/problem**

> > *Are there divided loyalties?*

> > *Is it an ethical or values dilemma?*

> **Gather the facts**

> > *Do you have the information you need?*

> > *Is it necessary to involve other parties?*

> **Test the options**

> > *Is the option legal?*

> > *Is it beneficial? detrimental?*

> > *What are short-term versus long-term consequences?*

> > *Do the benefits outweigh any potential harm?*

> > *Is it right?*

> > *How will it be perceived by others?*

> > *Could it embarrass your organization?*

> **Make a decision**

> **Share the decision with those directly involved**

A good manager knows how to set up win-win situations and keep everyone moving toward the goals. But learning this skill takes the ability to compromise and consider many perspectives at the same time. When negotiating:

➤ Always know what your high and low expectations are

➤ Tackle the easy issues first

➤ Be prepared to change your mind

➤ Leave yourself a way out

➤ Allow time to identify your options

➤ Make sure each party feels as if something has been gained

➤ Use persuasion, not intimidation

➤ Be patient

➤ Hold your temper

➤ Listen

➤ Resolve any conflicts that arise

➤ Seek common ground

Never make promises you cannot keep.
Never lie.
Never assume anything.

NEGOTIATING SELF-ASSESSMENT

1. With which people at work are you most likely to negotiate with?

_____

_____

2. With whom do you find it easiest to negotiate? Why?

_____

_____

3. Are there people you cannot negotiate with? Why?

_____

_____

Creating Win-Win Negotiations

The following six steps are common to most successful negotiations. Keep them in mind before you begin your next negotiation.

Step 1:

Get to know the party you will be negotiating with. Keep your initial interactions friendly, relaxed, and business-like.

Step 2:

Study all issues before negotiations begin. Be prepared to share your goals and objectives with the other party. Wait for their feedback to determine if there are differences. The atmosphere should be cooperative and trusting.

Step 3:

Raise specific issues to start the process. Obtain a consensus about splitting or combining issues and begin dealing with them one by one.

Step 4:

Express areas of agreement or conflict.

Step 5:

Reassess your position and decide what level of compromise is acceptable.

Step 6:

Affirm agreements and put them in writing.

Adapted from Negotiation Basics *by Robert B. Maddux and Charles Lickson, Crisp Series.*

Negotiations Worksheet

1. What are the goals, issues, problems, and/or targets that need negotiating?

   _____

   _____

2. What is the timing?

   _____

   _____

3. Do you need to offer an inspection? Product? Facility? Service? To what extent?

   _____

   _____

4. Who is involved?

   _____

   _____

5. Who has the authority to make the decisions?

   _____

   _____

CONTINUED

6. How much flexibility do you have?

   For example: How much are you willing to spend or sell for? What concessions are you willing to take or ask for?

   _____

   _____

7. What is your opening offer? Opening questions? What response strategies do you have that will move you closer to your goals?

   _____

   _____

8. What is your relationship to the party with whom you are negotiating?

   _____

   _____

9. What do you want your relationship to be after negotiations end?

   _____

   _____

Managing Conflict in the Workplace

Even if everyone has agreed on a goal, disagreements can occur. Here are seven suggestions for resolving conflicts:

1. Schedule a meeting with the other person to discuss the situation.

2. When you meet, acknowledge there is a conflict.

3. Use "I" statements to avoid accusations. Make sure the other person uses "I" statements too. For example, "I feel we are not together on the email policy. What do you think?"

4. Ask questions that require the other person to talk about the situation. Good questions start with, "Would you tell me your ideas for handling email?"

5. Repeat what you are being told: "You're telling me that we need a new policy?" is a good way to confirm that you understand what you are hearing.

6. State what each of you wants as an outcome.

7. Agree on a resolution and schedule a meeting to follow up on the situation.

To prevent conflict from escalating:

➤ Study the problem

➤ Do more listening than talking

➤ See the total solution

➤ Ask questions to find out the real meaning of words

➤ Avoid making moral judgments

➤ Try to empathize

➤ Put problems on the back burner if solutions aren't obvious

CONFLICT MANAGEMENT SELF-ASSESSMENT

Do you avoid giving negative feedback?

❏ Yes   ❏ No   ❏ Sometimes

If you answered "yes" or "sometimes," you may be encouraging office conflicts. Problems don't go away by avoiding them; they tend to escalate. Hone your communication skills so that you can frame criticism as positively as possible to motivate the person to change his or her behavior.

Do you react with anger when a conflict arises?

❏ Yes   ❏ No   ❏ Sometimes

Anger can be a double-edged sword. Used sparingly, it can be effective, but used often and indiscriminately, it will damage your reputation and lose you the respect of others. Control your anger by taking deep breaths, going for a walk, or talking it out with a confidante who is not a co-worker. If you lose your temper and act inappropriately, be prepared to apologize for your behavior, not your feelings of anger. If you are dealing with an angry employee, customer, or peer, allow the person to blow off steam, but within reason. Firmly and immediately stop any tirade or abuse.

Do you blame others for their problems?

❏ Yes   ❏ No   ❏ Sometimes

When you place blame, you put your attention in the wrong place. Blame wastes time and does not address the real problem or its solution. When you place blame on someone, you surrender authority and control. Instead of playing blame games, assess the situation and define solutions. Make sure people are accountable for their actions and the results of their actions. Take corrective action to improve performance, but never place blame.

Dealing with Difficult People

Difficult people can be negative, irritating, and too often, seemingly impossible to deal with—and they create stress for everyone around them. They can be employees, customers, co-workers, peers, and managers.

When you can assess the person's behavior and really listen to what is said, you can more effectively handle a difficult personality.

Follow these strategies for dealing with the seven basic types of difficult people:

Attackers

Attackers charge and need room and time to blow off steam. Get them into a private area, address them by name and listen to their position. Don't argue or get in a shouting match; ask them to calm down and present your response in a firm, calm way.

Egotists

Egotists also come on strong, but unlike attackers, they often act like subject experts. Respect their knowledge and ask questions, but don't allow them to "take over."

Sneaks

Sneaks often use sarcasm or underhanded means of getting what they want. Your best defense is to expose them with direct questions about what bothers them. They often retreat if directly queried about what their sarcasm really means.

Victims

Victims act powerless and defeated, and often whine. Ask them for suggestions to improve the situation. Logically, refute their negative comments with facts.

Negators

Negators are usually suspicious of those in authority and believe that their opinion is the only legitimate one. Let negators "vent" before focusing on real solutions.

Super-Agreeable People

Super-agreeable people want to be liked and offer to do whatever you want them to do. They overcommit themselves and often disappoint and frustrate others. Monitor what they volunteer to do to make sure they aren't overworked. Disassociate actions from their sense of self-worth.

Unresponsive People

Unresponsive people are withdrawn and it is seemingly impossible to gain a positive commitment from them. Try using more open-ended, indirect questions and wait for them to respond. Resist the urge to finish sentences for them. Give them tasks that require reports at regular intervals.

Managing Change

Change is inevitable. Computers, the Internet, electronic advances, reorganizations, downsizing. It all means change. As a manager, you must be prepared to help people accept and adapt to change. In the words of Machiavelli, "There is nothing more difficult to take in hand, more perilous to conduct, or more uncertain in its success, than to take the lead in introducing a new order of things."

Employees may like business as usual. They feel secure with the familiar. Often change stimulates basic fears such as loss of control, uncertainty, surprise, and having to take on more work. Change is often greeted with resistance, excuses, escape, and reasons for why it won't work. But change can offer opportunity. Change is necessary for survival. Organizations must change to remain competitive. The playing field is never level for long, and managers must take a lead in coping with and helping their employees through change.

Successful change is built in small steps.

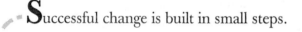

CHANGE WORKSHEET

The following worksheet will help you implement change effectively.

Who initiated the change?

_____

_____

What is the nature of the change?

_____

_____

What follow-up actions will be required?

_____

_____

Who will be the primary change agent?

_____

_____

Who needs to be involved in the change process?

_____

_____

Who needs to be informed of the change?

_____

_____

CONTINUED

What personnel problems might the change create?

_____

_____

How will I inform my office about the change?

_____

_____

How will others be affected?

_____

_____

How will I know I have been successful in helping implement the change?

_____

_____

What details about the change need to be communicated?

_____

_____

When will each step be completed?

_____

_____

When can I expect the change to be in place?

_____

_____

The Importance of Good Customer Relations

> "No customer can be worse than no customer."
>
> —Leon Fechtner

Everybody Is a Customer

In a truly service-driven organization, everybody and every unit has a customer. If you or the members of your unit never see the customers, you still have internal customers of your own. Your customers are the people who depend on you, wholly or in part, to get their jobs done. All of the functions and departments of a service business are interlinked, and each one depends on others to various degrees in accomplishing its mission.

Customer service definition ⎯⎯⎯⎯⎯⎯⎯⎯⎯⎯

Whatever enhances a customer's satisfaction through meeting his or her expectations and needs.

Understanding Customer Needs

Most businesses are designed to support customers or clients, whether they are external, or internal (i.e. other departments). In any case, good customer relation skills are essential. Customer survey research indicates that there are four basic customer needs.

Customers want to:

1. Be understood

2. Feel welcome and comfortable

3. Feel important and respected

4. Have their needs met

Adapted from Quality Customer Service, *by William Martin, Crisp Series.*

Creating a Customer-First Environment

Step 1   Encourage staff to develop a genuine interest in customers or co-workers and their well-being. Define quality service at various points of contact.

Step 2   Develop an atmosphere of openness, honesty, and integrity.

Step 3   Identify all of your customers and their needs.

Step 4   Analyze your services and cite areas to improve.

Step 5   Practice problem-solving techniques. Do not tolerate pressuring, controlling, or manipulating.

Complaint-Solving Model

Try using this six-step process to solve complaints.

Step 1   Empathize. Acknowledge the person's feelings.

Step 2   Apologize if appropriate and state that you want to help.

Step 3   Probe for further information.

Step 4   Repeat the person's concern to make sure you've understood.

Step 5   Explain options or actions you will take to correct the problem.

Step 6   Restate your position and end pleasantly.

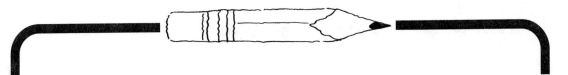

COMPLAINT-SOLVING EXERCISE

In the following exercise you will use the six-step process to solve complaints. Identify what is wrong with each employee response and, using the six steps, describe what the appropriate response should be.

Situation 1

Customer:
"Why must I pay a $10 returned check fee because someone gave me a bad check and my account went overdrawn? It's not my fault."

Employee:
"Because those are the rules."

Your response: (Hint: try Step 1)

_____

_____

Situation 2

Customer:
"Why are your prices higher than your competitors?"

Employee:
"I don't think they are high."

Your response: (Hint: try Step 4)

_____

_____

CONTINUED

CONTINUED

Situation 3

Customer: "You were supposed to come this morning and I've been waiting all day!"

Employee: "Our truck broke down and we're behind schedule."

Your response: (Hint: try Step 1)

_____

_____

Situation 4

Customer: "Why did you deny my claim? My doctor ordered this?"

Employee: "It's not covered under your contract."

Your response: (Hint: try Steps 1 & 6)

_____

_____

Situation 5

Customer: "I bought this at one of your stores. Can I return it here?"

Employee: "No."

Your response: (Hint: try Step 5)

_____

_____

Compare your answers to the authors' suggestions on page 101

PROFESSIONAL DEVELOPMENT REVIEW

Answer the following questions as honestly as possible. Use them to help you apply what you have learned from this book.

1. What are your personal goals?

_____

_____

_____

2. What are you professional office goals?

_____

_____

_____

3. What skills have you recently learned to help you achieve both personal and professional goals?

Personal:

_____

_____

Professional:

_____

_____

4. What training have you taken that can make you a more professional office manager?

_____

_____

Professional Development Review (continued)

5. What training have you given your employees to help your office be more productive?

_____

_____

6. What training are you planning over the next year?

_____

_____

7. How will this training contribute to your goals?

_____

_____

8. How do you plan to apply to your office what you have learned from this book?

_____

_____

AUTHORS' SUGGESTED RESPONSES TO COMPLAINT-SOLVING EXERCISE (P. 97-98)

Your specific responses will vary, but here are the authors' suggestions for handling these complaints.

Situation 1

Using Step 1, start by acknowledging the customer's feelings: "I can understand your frustration. It probably doesn't seem fair."

Situation 2

Use Step 5 to try to satisfy customer: "Prices can vary according to services provided. Let's look at the specific services you need…"

Situation 3

Use Step 1 to acknowledge the customer's feelings: "I'm sorry you were inconvenienced. It's so frustrating when an unexpected delay happens."

Situation 4

Use Step 1 to diffuse the customer's frustration and anger, and then use Step 6 to explain the situation: "You must feel upset about this, let me clarify a few points about your coverage…"

Situation 5

Use Step 5 to try to help the customer: "We don't carry the same stock at each store. Let me check with our central office about how to best handle this."

Additional Reading

Bonet, Diana. *The Business of Listening*. Crisp Series, 2001.

Conrad, Pamela J. and Robert B. Maddux. *A Guide to Affirmative Action*. Crisp Series, 1997.

Haynes, Marion E. *Project Management*. Crisp Series, 2002.

Maddux, Robert B. *Performance Management*. Crisp Series, 2000.

Maddux, Robert B. and Charles Lickson. *Negotiation Basics*. Crisp Series, 2005.

Maddux, Robert B. *Quality Interviewing*. Crisp Series, 1995.

Manning, Marilyn and Carolyn Barnes. *Professionalism in the Office*. Crisp Series, 2001.

Manning, Marilyn and Patricia Haddock. *Leadership Skills for Women*. Crisp Series, 1995.

Minor, Marianne A. *Coaching and Counseling*. Crisp Series, 2002.

Pollar, Odette and Rafael Gonzales. *Dynamics of Diversity: Strategic Programs for Your Organization*. Crisp Series, 1995.

Zaccarelli, Herman E. *Training Managers to Train*. Crisp Series, 2004.

Also Available

Books•Videos•Computer-Based Training Products

If you enjoyed this book, we have great news for you. There are over 200 books available in the *Crisp Fifty-Minute™ Series*. For more information visit us online at www.courseilt.com

Subject Areas Include:

Management

Human Resources

Communication Skills

Personal Development

Sales/Marketing

Finance

Coaching and Mentoring

Customer Service/Quality

Small Business and Entrepreneurship

Training

Life Planning

Writing

VERP